W9-AEG-813

ED EMBERLEY'S DRAWING BOOK

OF ANIMALS

LITTLE, BROWN AND COMPANY
BOSTON · NEW YORK · LONDON

OTHER BOOKS BY ED EMBERLEY:

ED EMBERLEY'S DRAWING BOOK OF FACES
ED EMBERLEY'S DRAWING BOOK: MAKE A WORLD
ED EMBERLEY'S GREAT THUMBPRINT DRAWING BOOK
ED EMBERLEY'S PICTURE PIE: A CIRCLE DRAWING BOOK

COPYRIGHT © 1970 BY EDWARD R. EMBERLEY
ALL RIGHTS RESERVED. NO PART OF THIS BOOK MAY BE REPRODUCED IN ANY FORM OR BY ANY
ELECTRONIC OR MECHANICAL MEANS, INCLUDING INFORMATION STORAGE AND
RETRIEVAL SYSTEMS WITHOUT PERMISSION IN WRITING FROM THE PUBLISHER,
EXCEPT BY A REVIEWER, WHO MAY QUOTE BRIEF PASSAGES IN A REVIEW.
FIRST PAPERBACK EDITION
10 9 8
WOR
PRINTED IN THE UNITED STATES OF AMERICA

FOR THE BOY I WAS,
THE BOOK I COULD NOT FIND

IF YOU CAN DRAW THESE SHAPES, LETTERS, NUMBERS AND THINGS →

YOU WILL BE ABLE TO DRAW ALL THE ANIMALS IN THIS BOOK.

FOR INSTANCE :

IN ORDER TO DRAW THIS POLLYWOG ~⚫ YOU USE THESE ⚫ S · |

IN ORDER TO DRAW THIS BIRD 🐦 YOU USE THESE ⭕ D ▲▲ · ||| ∨∨

THE DIAGRAMS ON THE FOLLOWING PAGES

WILL SHOW YOU HOW. *Happy drawing, Ed Emberley*

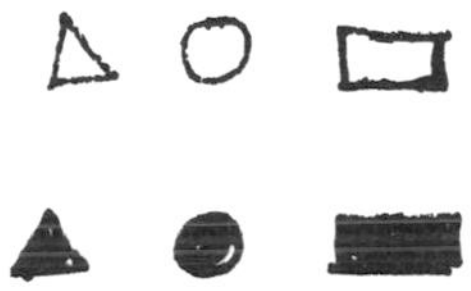

SHAPES

Y J L

C D S

V W M

U

LETTERS

1 2 3

NUMBERS

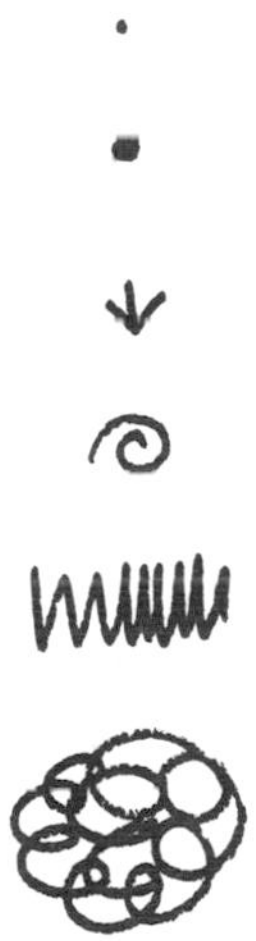

SMALL DOT

LARGE DOT

BIRD TRACK

CURLICUE

SCRATCHY SCRIBBLE

CURLY SCRIBBLE

THINGS

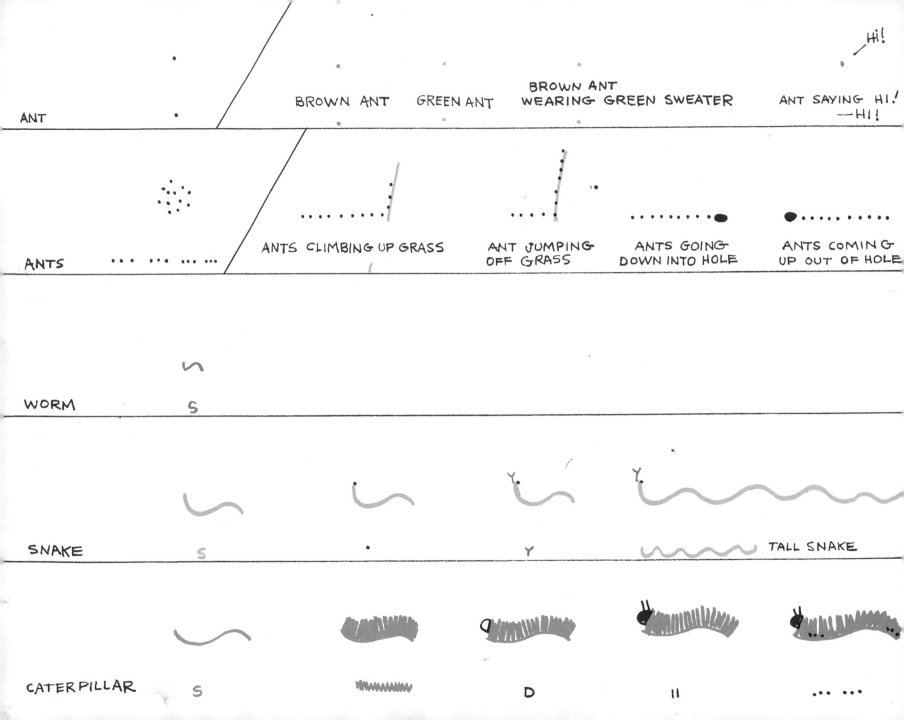

ANT

BROWN ANT GREEN ANT

BROWN ANT
WEARING GREEN SWEATER

ANT SAYING HI!
—HI!

Hi!

ANTS

ANTS CLIMBING UP GRASS

ANT JUMPING
OFF GRASS

ANTS GOING
DOWN INTO HOLE

ANTS COMING
UP OUT OF HOLE

WORM

S

SNAKE

S   Y   TALL SNAKE

CATERPILLAR

S   D   II   ... ...

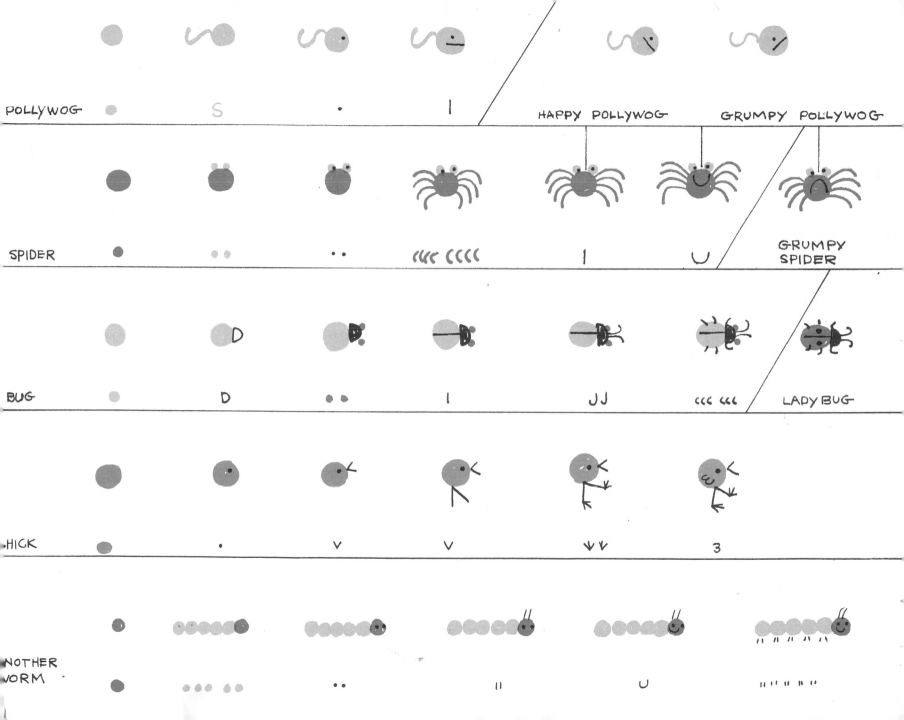

POLLYWOG   S   .   I   HAPPY POLLYWOG   GRUMPY POLLYWOG

SPIDER   .   ..   ..   (((((((I   U   GRUMPY
SPIDER

BUG   D   ..   I   JJ   ((((((LADY BUG

HICK   .   V   V   V V   3

NOTHER
VORM   II   U   " " " " "

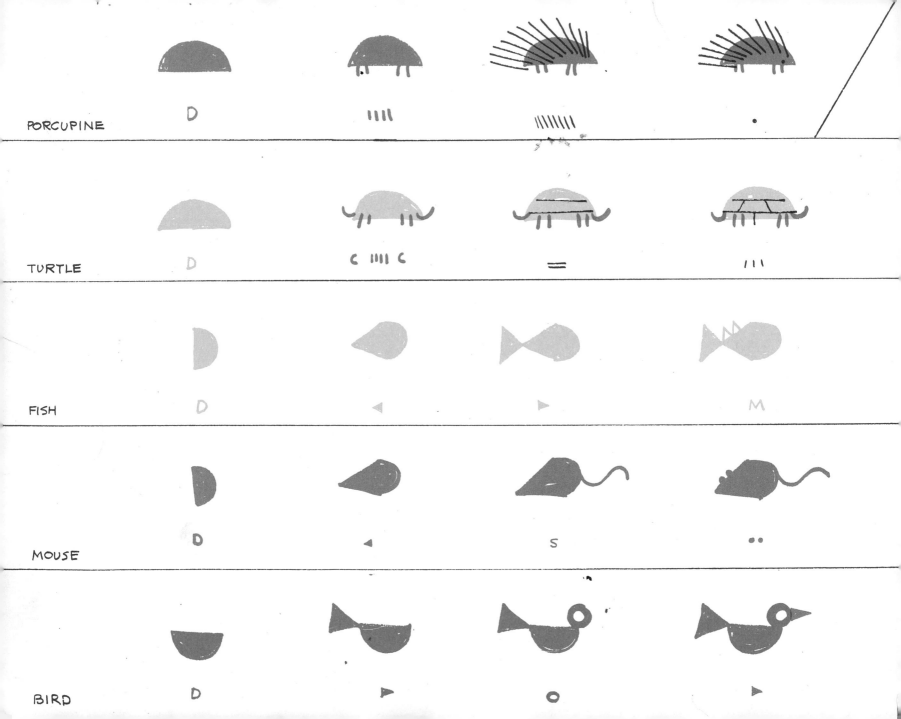

PORCUPINE

TURTLE

FISH

MOUSE

BIRD

PORCUPINE SITTING   PORCUPINE SLEEPING   PORCUPINE JUMPING OVER A STONE

TURTLE SLEEPING   TURTLE DANCING   TURTLE SKATING IN THE RAIN

W   .   I   FISH SWIMMING ON HIS BACK

" "   . ||| ||| •   MOUSE, TOP VIEW

| || •   ∨ ∨   3

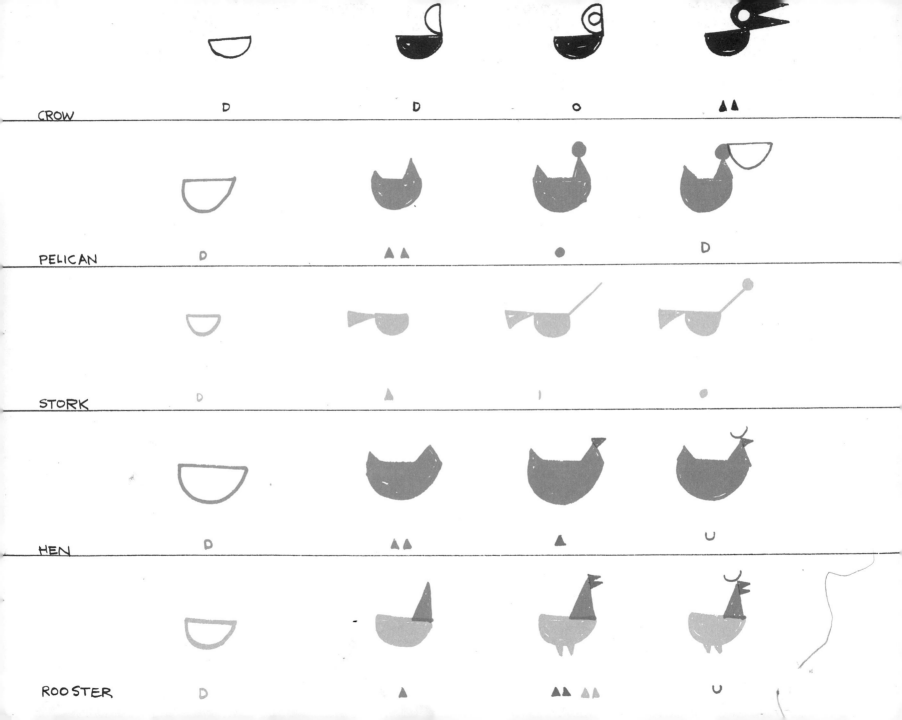

CROW

PELICAN

STORK

HEN

ROOSTER

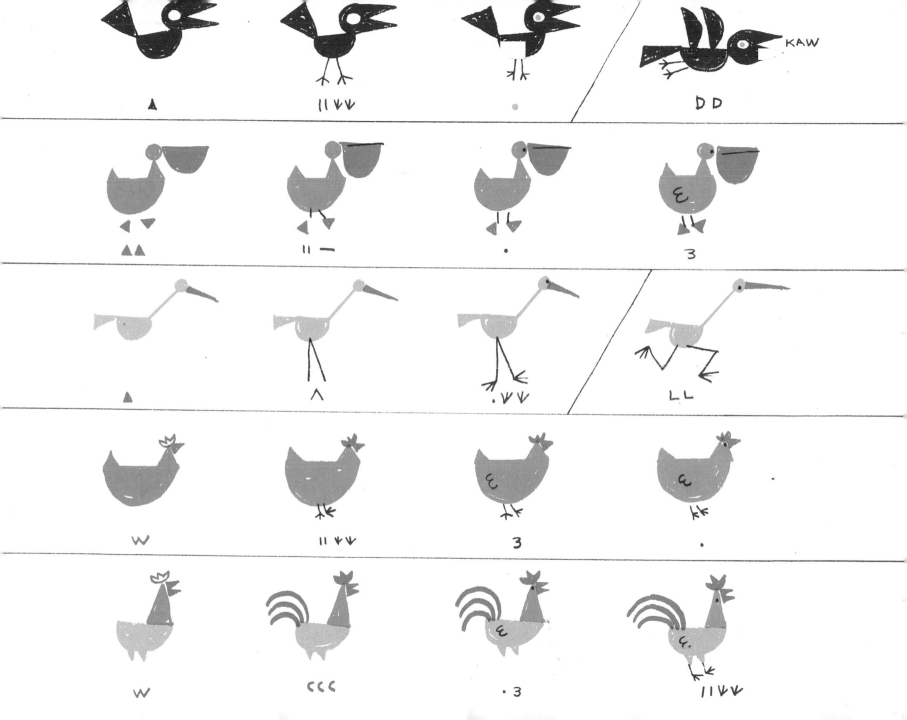

A   II ⇓⇓   ·   D D   KAW

▲▲   II —   ·   3

▲   ∧   ·⇓⇓   L L

W   II ⇓⇓   3   ·

W   CCC   ·3   II ⇓⇓

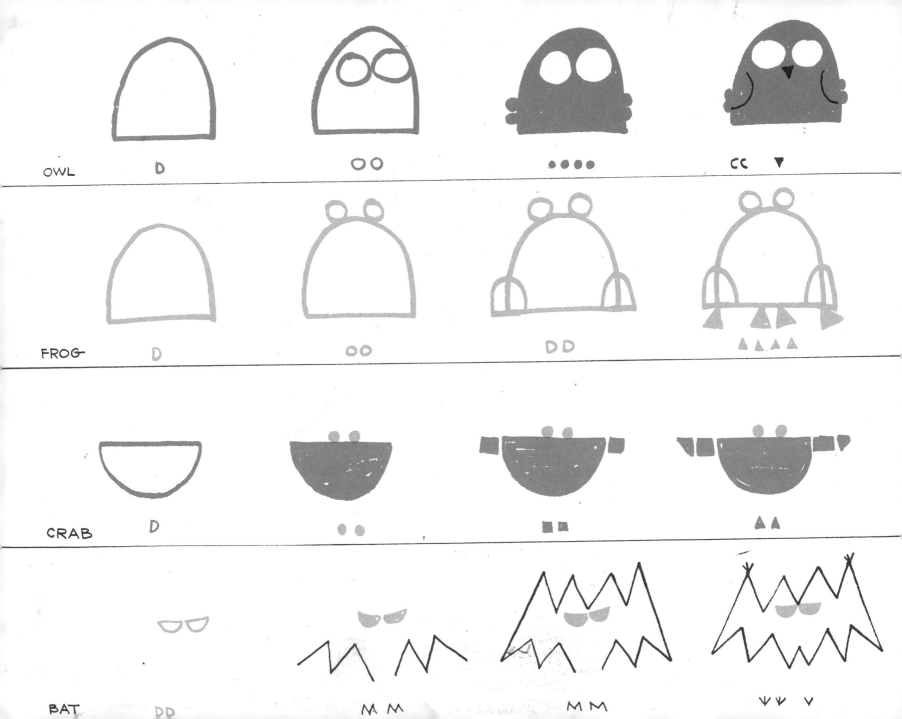

OWL   D   OO   ••••   CC ▼

FROG   D   OO   DD   ▲▲▲▲

CRAB   D   ●●   ■■   ▲▲

BAT   DD   M M   M M   Ѵ Ѵ Ѵ

|| ↓↓   333   • •   ▷— •∨

|| ∪   • • ••   CROAKING FROG   SLEEPING FROG

 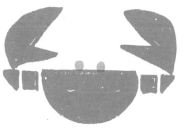  

ᗪ ᗪ   ▲ ▲   ((( )))   JJ

• • | BAT, BACK VIEW   BABY BAT

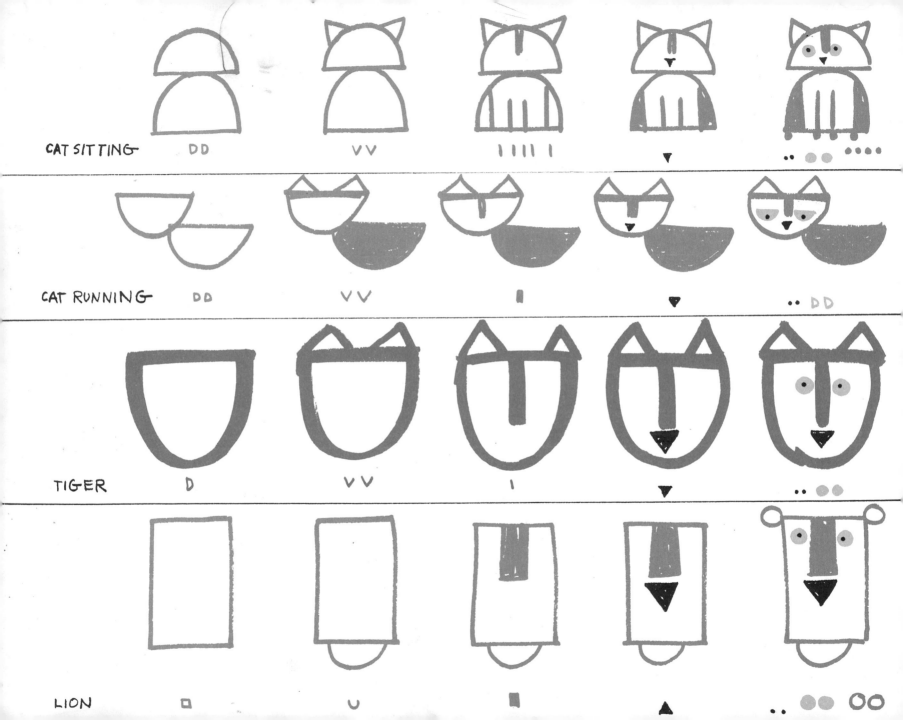

CAT SITTING DD VV I I I I I I ▼ .. ● ● ● ● ● ●

CAT RUNNING DD VV I ▼ .. DD

TIGER D VV I ▼ .. ● ●

LION □ ∪ ▮ ▲ .. ● ● ○ ○

UU   J   III III   FAT CAT

J CCCC   ,,,,, ,,, ,,, ,,, I   ,, CCC CCC   BLACK CAT RUNNING THE OTHER WAY

Y   //// //// //   ▲▲▲▲▲▲▲▲▲▲▲▲

Y   VVV   //// ////   uuuu

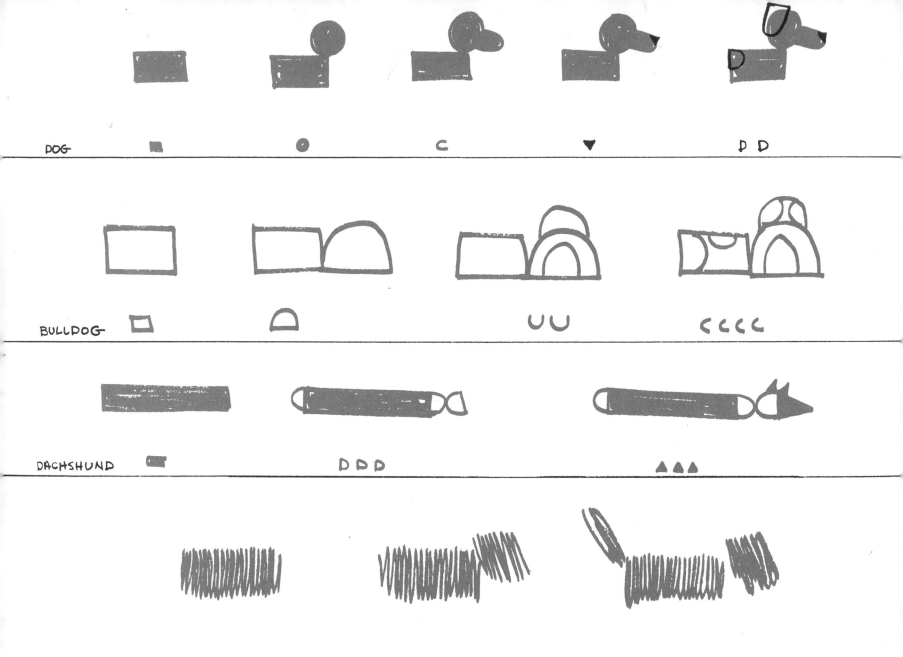

DOG

BULLDOG

DACHSHUND

SHAGGY DOG   SCRIBBLE   SCRIBBLE   SCRIBBLE

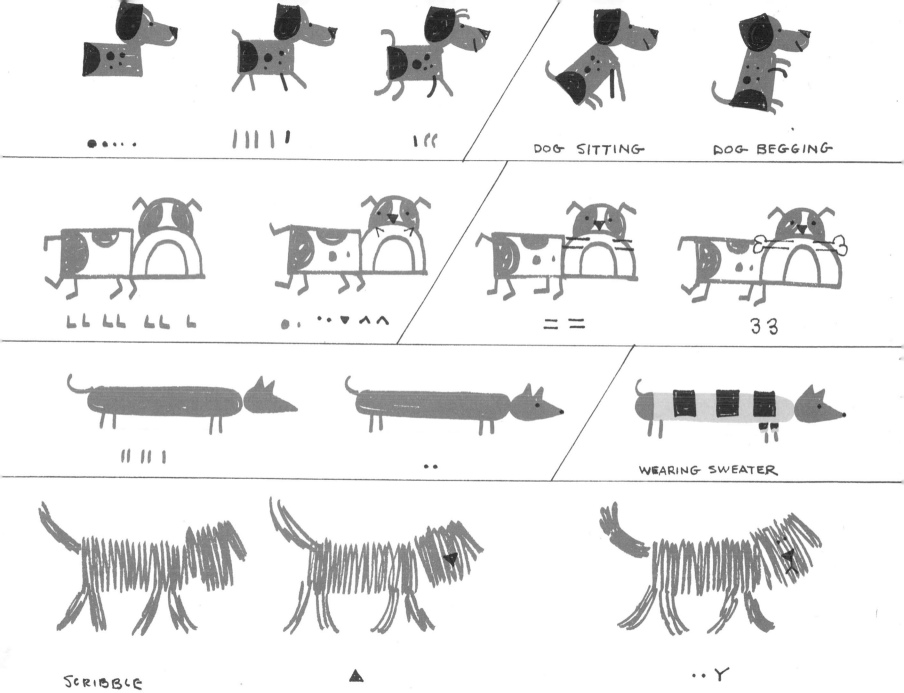

DOG SITTING

DOG BEGGING

WEARING SWEATER

SCRIBBLE

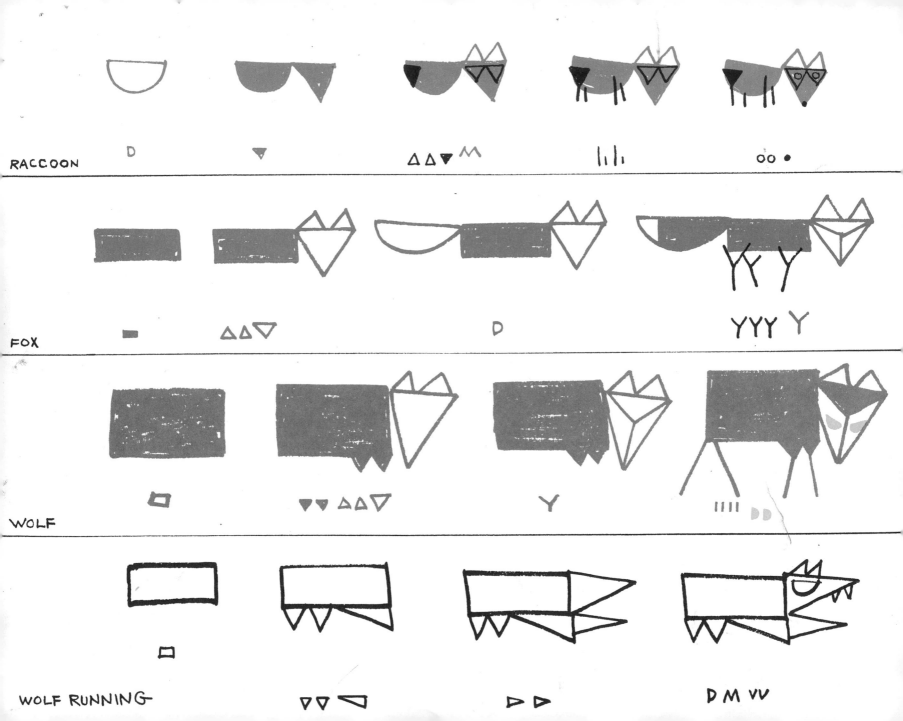

RACCOON

FOX

WOLF

WOLF RUNNING

..

D

|||||

C

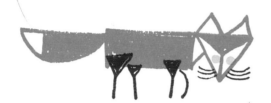

/ ((((((

....

... S

S ||| ||| || /// ///

WOLF LOOKING THE OTHER WAY

||||| .

S ((((|||| .

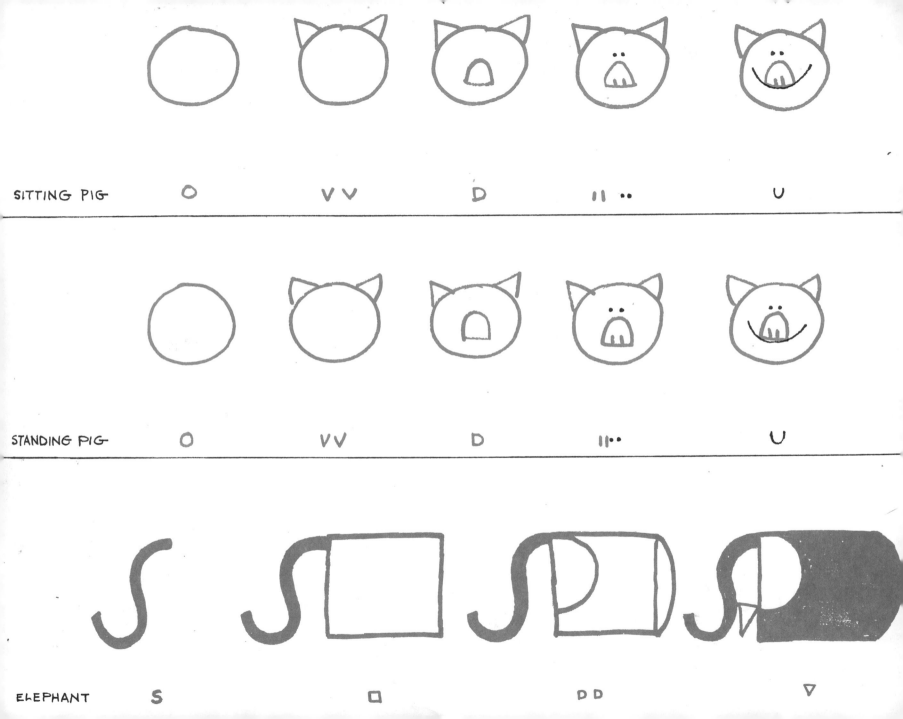

SITTING PIG   O   V V   D   ll ••   U

STANDING PIG   O   V V   D   ll••   U

ELEPHANT   S   □   D D   ▽

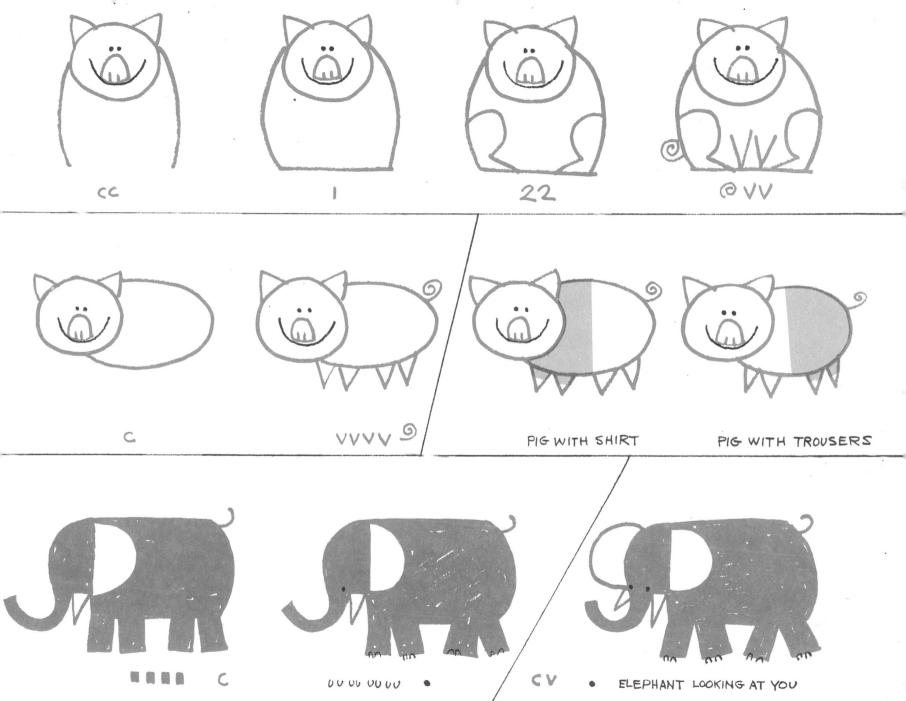

cc

1

22

@ VV

c

VVVV @

PIG WITH SHIRT

PIG WITH TROUSERS

⬛⬛⬛⬛ C

U U UU UU UU •

CV •   ELEPHANT LOOKING AT YOU

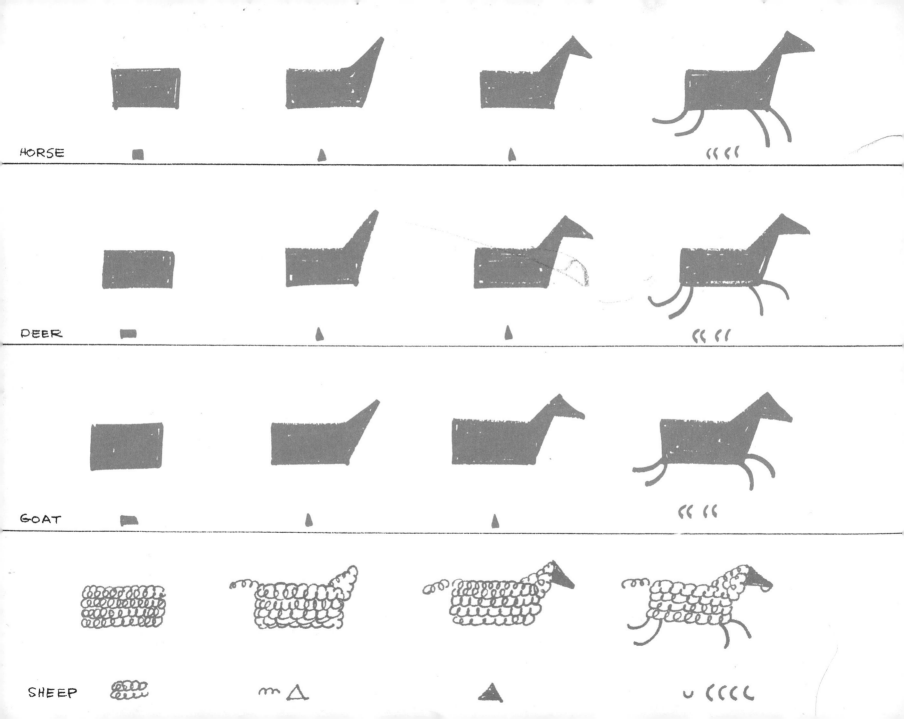

HORSE

DEER

GOAT

SHEEP

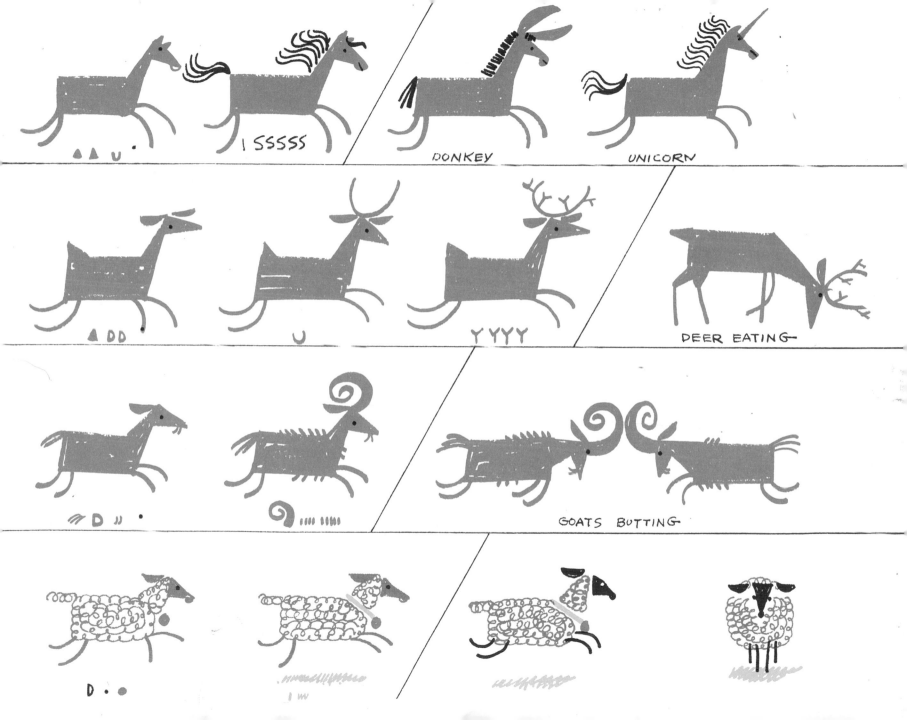

I SSSSS

DONKEY

UNICORN

DEER EATING

GOATS BUTTING

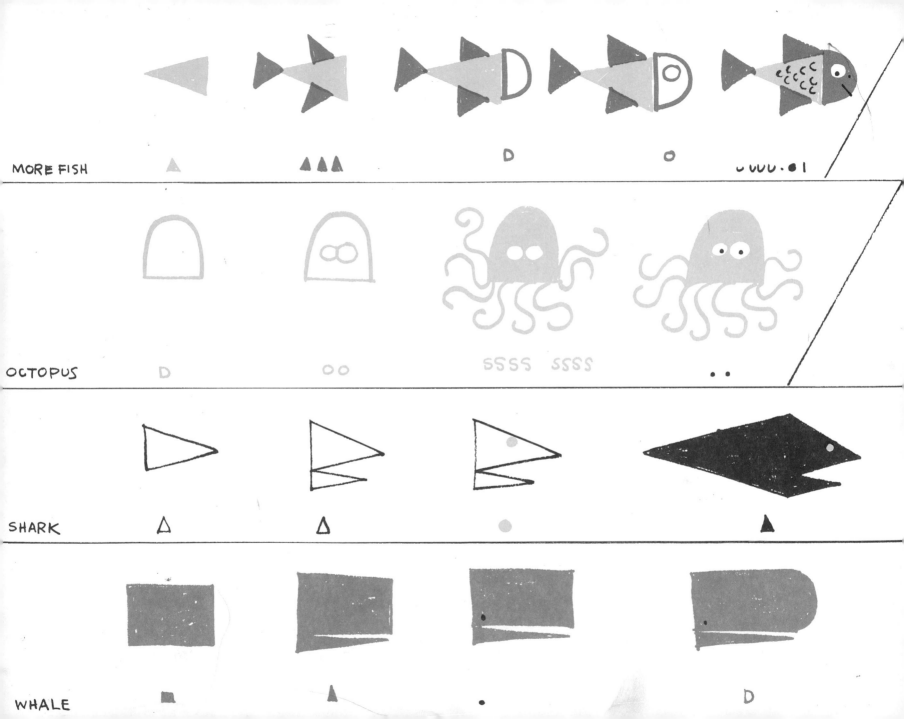

MORE FISH

OCTOPUS

SHARK

WHALE

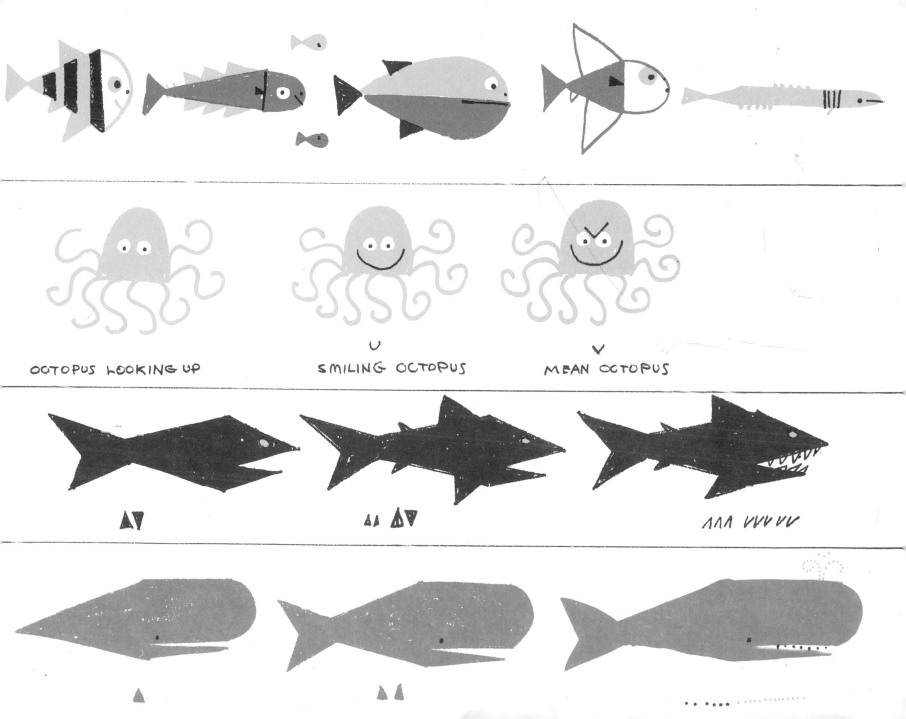

OCTOPUS LOOKING UP SMILING OCTOPUS MEAN OCTOPUS

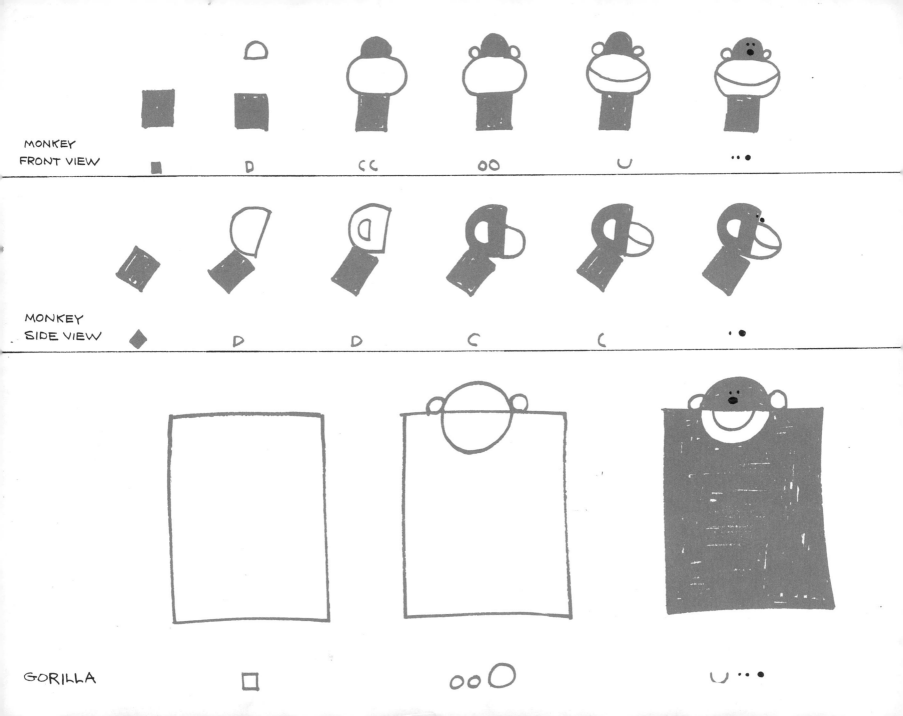

MONKEY
FRONT VIEW

MONKEY
SIDE VIEW

GORILLA

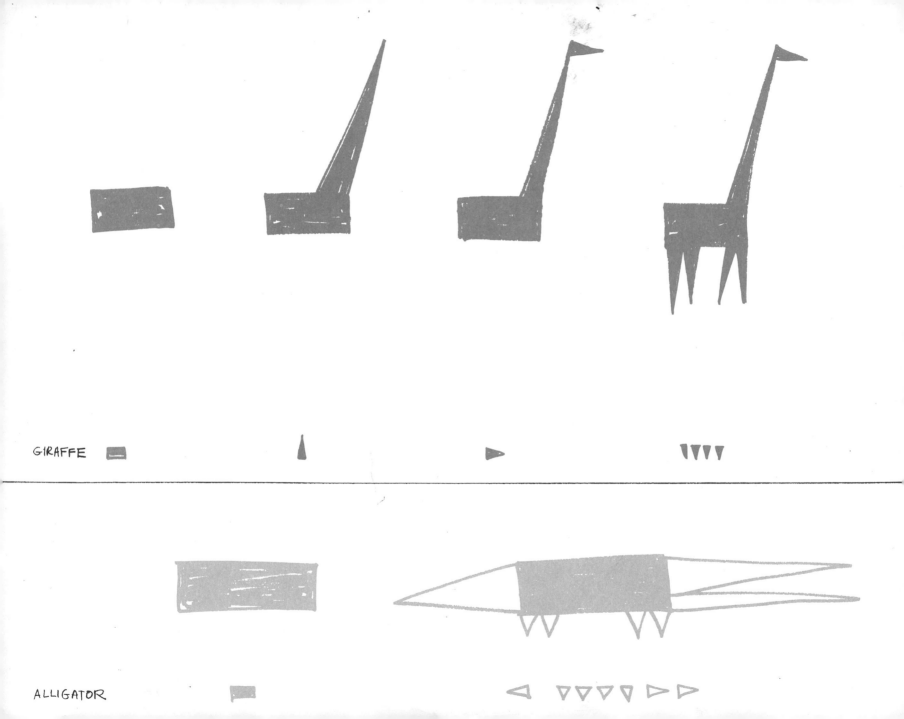

GIRAFFE

ALLIGATOR

DRAGON   D   SSS   SS

▲▲   VV VV I   VV ,,,   ●● ○○   SS   CC

// // // MM V   ▲▲ ▲▲▲▲▲▲▲▲ ▲▲▲   ..

THERE ARE MANY WAYS YOU CAN
CHANGE THE BASIC DRAWINGS.
YOU CAN...

YOU CAN MAKE PEOPLE AND ANIMALS
LOOK SAD, HAPPY, MEAN, EMBARRASSED OR
GRUMPY BY CHANGING THEIR
EYEBROWS AND/OR MOUTHS, LIKE THIS...

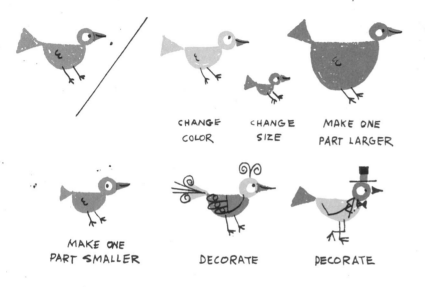

CHANGE COLOR   CHANGE SIZE   MAKE ONE PART LARGER

MAKE ONE PART SMALLER   DECORATE   DECORATE

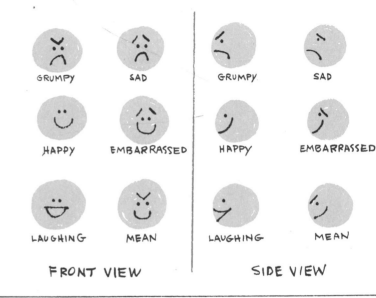

GRUMPY	SAD	GRUMPY	SAD
HAPPY	EMBARRASSED	HAPPY	EMBARRASSED
LAUGHING	MEAN	LAUGHING	MEAN

FRONT VIEW   SIDE VIEW

PECKING   LOOKING UP   LOOKING BACK

SITTING   SINGING   RUNNING

YOU CAN USE THIS SIMPLE METHOD OF
DRAWING TO BLOCK IN MORE COMPLICATED
DRAWINGS. FOR INSTANCE...

BLOCK IN   FILL IN   EMBELLISH